DAUGHTERS

Balestier Press
Centurion House, London TW18 4AX
www.balestier.com

Daughters
Original title: 女兒
Copyright © Ling Yü, 2022
English translation © Nicholas Y. H. Wong, 2025

First published in Chinese by
Ink Literary Monthly Publishing Co., Ltd. (Taiwan) in 2022.

This English edition first published by Balestier Press in 2025.

Published with the support of the Ministry of Culture, Taiwan.

A CIP catalogue record for this book is available from the British Library.

ISBN 978 1 913891 68 8

All rights reserved. No part of this publication may be reproduced, stored in a retrieval system, or transmitted in any form or by any means, electronic or mechanical, without prior written permission from the publisher.

LING YÜ

DAUGHTERS

Translated from the Chinese by
Nicholas Y. H. Wong

BALESTIER PRESS
LONDON · SINGAPORE

Contents

Translator's Preface 7

I
East Coast 17
The Sea is My Name 18
Daughters 28

II
And Then Later 39
My Mother who is a Centenarian . . 41
Swap 42
White 44
All Her Life 46
Without Hope 47
Freeze 49
Sew 50
How Come My 51
A Christening 53
Language *for M* 55
Photograph 57
Just the Same 59
A House of a Kind 61
New and Old 63
Isn't That 64
Hereafter 66

What Each Family Has . . . 67
Alms Bowl 69
Talking to Prisoners 70
Dreams 72

III

Z and Me 75
   Midway 77, Thirty Years 78, Cactus 80, Civilized 82,
   Half 84, That Celestial Body 85, Cross-examination 86,
   Myth 87, Language 88, Dreaming and Waking 89,
   Betrayal 91, Cracks 92, The Other Side 93,
   Rooftop 95, Two Lamps 96, Olive Trees 97,
   The Years 98, Banishment 99, Pay no Mind 101,
   Hide and Seek 103, Cut to Shreds 105, Old Age 106,
   Teardrops 108, Sound 109, Stagger 111, Dusk 113,
   I Like 115, The Depths 117

IV

Looking at Pictures—Utagawa Hiroshige's
   Fifty-Three Stations of the Tōkaidō . . 119

Epilogue 131
Translator's Afterword: A Poet's Wanderlusting Blue 137
About the Translator 145

Translator's Preface

WINNER OF THE 2025 NEWMAN PRIZE for Chinese Literature, Ling Yü (零雨, pen name of Wang Mei-chin 王美琴) was born in 1952 in the district of Pinglin in southeastern New Taipei, Taiwan. Ling Yü's works "span themes of meditation, travel, feminism, capitalism, the environment, mythology and more" by employing "classical and modern, Eastern and Western literary, philosophical, artistic, and esoteric sources," according to Cosima Bruno's prize citation. Even the name Ling Yü is a heady mix of classical tradition and plain life experienced as a quiet shower. It means *fine rain*, taken from the oldest extant collection of Chinese poetry, *Book of Songs*, which dates to the 7th–11th century BC, "representing all that is contradictory and also the inner conflicts" in Ling Yü's poems. Deeply influenced by Taoism, Ling Yü writes spontaneously: "guided by the moment," which is how she "understands the fundamental value of life," Ling Yü "only writes when it comes naturally, not for the sake of writing." Or, as Ling Yü recounted, after reading Plato's dialogue *Phaedrus* with her friends, her writing captures what Plato calls "Dionysian frenzy."[1] *Daughters* (2022), here translated, is Ling Yü's ninth poetry collection, not counting the two bilingual Collected Works. Its tender response to caring for her aging mother is brought into focus by other effortless poems about love and meditations on art.

---

[1] "2023 La Nuit de la Littérature" [2023 Night of Literature]. https://www.youtube.com/watch?v=VpxKjsW387M&t .

Daughters was awarded Taiwan's OpenBook Prize and Taiwan Literature Award's "Golden Book Prize" in 2022. In both acceptance speeches, Ling Yü refers to mothers and daughters in the same breath as the Japanese artist Utagawa Hiroshige's (1797–1858) "floating world" prints, known as *ukiyo-e* (浮世絵). *Daughters* ponders "questions about daughters in society, family values and ethics, groups and individuals. It is dedicated to my mother. The last section of *Daughters*, though, pays tribute to Hiroshige," an artist Ling Yü "considers a mother who gave birth to me, nourished me, and kept me company. So, *Daughters* is dedicated to mothers in a broad sense."[2] Note here that Ling Yü calls Hiroshige *mother* rather than *father*. In the second speech, Ling Yü yet again connects familial roles to individual artistic inspiration. Literary forms help Ling Yü transcend norms in patriarchal society: "Daughters, multiple in this book, represent different experiences of wretched loneliness and helplessness from this era. I hope to convey the idea that the weak can similarly stand up to or communicate their hardships in life. Utagawa Hiroshige's *The Fifty-three Stations of the Tōkaidō* (東海道五十三次) might seem like individual *ukiyo-e* prints, but they contain traits commonly found in Chinese ink wash paintings. They made me feel a certain way, so I thought of writing poems for them."[3] Ling Yü's choice of making *style* out of gendered tradition deserves attention. In my translations, I match the elegant concision of her classical references, but adopt a colloquial, pithy tone in English when the poem's speaker redresses romantic and family dynamics, to express Ling Yü's balance in the

---

[2] "2022 Openbook haoshu jiang, niandu Zhongwen chuangzuo *Nüer* zuozhe Ling Yü dejiang ganyan" [2022 OpenBook prize for Chinese-language writing every year. Acceptance speech by Ling Yü, author of *Daughters*]. https://www.youtube.com/watch?v=tUzPbQnwCUE .

[3] "2022 Taiwan wenxue jiang jindian jiang | Ling Yü *Nüer*" [2022 Taiwan Literature Award's Golden Book Prize | Ling Yü's *Daughters*]. https://www.youtube.com/watch?v=tSsuBsyz-CA .

continuum of life and art.

Daughter's eponymous ten-poem sequence, "Daughters," is now repurposed into song by the singer Lo Sirong (羅思容) for a forthcoming video-poem by Fisfisa Media (目宿媒體). Poetic lines move across *dimensions* (次元), a Japanese loanword that Ling Yü uses in "Epilogue," from art prints to word to video, laying bare the transmedial possibilities of Ling Yü's thinking about gender. Audiences at Poetry International Festival Rotterdam and Hong Kong International Poetry Nights have heard Ling Yü's poems read aloud. Now they are also visualized song-texts.

Like *Daughters*, Ling Yü's other poetry collections are thematically crafted. But they share a trust in poetic language's incessant energies to free nature and humanity from confined gendered spaces. In Ling Yü's first collection, *Series on a City* (城的連作, 1990), nature haunts depictions of city life. In *Names Disappearing on the Map* (消失在地圖上的名字, 1992), nature escapes the spatial metaphors of cages, rooms, windows, and corners. *Stunt Family* (特技家族, 1993) won Taiwan's Annual Poetry Award for depicting the boundaries between the alienating stunts of body language and human consciousness through portals like doors, corridors, and ropes, tracking spatial movement through light and darkness, presence and emptiness. *Mudong Hymns* (木冬歌詠集, 1999) delves into religion and proposes a feminine subject to imagine an androgynous Creator. *Some Calculations of a Hometown* (關於故鄉的一些計算, 2006) casts poetic language as protean creatures resembling deities, capable of renaming all things. *I'm Heading for You* (我正前往你, 2010) uses train imagery to reflect on capitalist modernity's collision course with the environment.

Ling Yü taught at National Ilan University from 1992 to 2021, and lives in Ilan, close to Taiwan's east coast, about an hour's drive to Taipei. *Idyll / 5.49 P.M.* (田園下午／五點四十九分, 2014), which won the Wu Zhuoliu Literary Award's New Poetry Honorable Mention (2015), depicts Ling Yü's scenic observations on her train journey back and forth between Taipei and Ilan. They mourn the lack of bucolic spaces in the wake of industrial capitalism. Primordial female consciousness brings forth new vocabulary through fragmentary reorganization. Finally, *Skin-Colored Time* (膚色的時光, 2018) pays homage to various artists and writers, and thus, as Ling Yü tells me, is a collection "written in blood and tears."[4] Cropping up in this volume are New Age beliefs such as *Seth Material* (1963–84) whereby Jane Roberts channels the spiritual being Seth and dictates his words to her husband. Spiritualists form the entourage of those who have inspired Ling Yü's work.

Ling Yü obtained her BA from the Chinese department in National Taiwan University, and an MA degree in East Asian studies from the University of Wisconsin-Madison. She was a visiting scholar at Harvard University in 1991. Ling Yü started writing poetry in 1983, after she had turned thirty. Chief editor for *Modern Poetry* (現代詩) from 1985 to 1991, Ling Yü co-founded the influential avant-garde journal *Poetry Now* (現在詩) in 2001, which ran till 2011, with poets like Hsia Yü and Hung Hung. Taken together, Ling Yü's editorial work and creative practice are defining forces in contemporary Chinese-language poetry and world poetry. It is my deep honor to present Ling Yü's *Daughters* in English.

Nicholas Y. H. Wong
January 2025

---

[4] Correspondence with the author, 20 January 2025.

For Mother

DAUGHTERS

I

East Coast

Powder blue greenish blue yellowish blue violet blue indigo blue
   bright blue ink blue light blue dark blue deep blue sky blue
Shuang-hsi blue Fulong blue Turtle Island blue Pacific Island blue
   Cawi' blue ukiyo blue bittersweet blue
A wanderlusting blue…

Ninety-nine types of blue

Windows
Facing the beach

Entering and leaving
My heart's color mixing tray

The Sea is My Name

1. Bus

A bus
Makes a detour along the beachfront fishing village

Without passengers, it looks worn out
About to disintegrate

He got on, became
A part of that emptiness

Just then, driving to the sea
Felt like parking in someone's courtyard

His heart and bus
Were shrouded in mist
Grayish, the sunset steered on—
Eventually he'd find a rest stop

—Under some lamplight in the village
He bypassed the dark
Before standing in the light

That darkness and light crisscrossed
Cast themselves on his body

He'd walked on those crossings
Quite slowly

But mustering strength led him
To the front of a house

2. Sleepless Tonight

I feel like I've been here
Before

He told the owner of the
Lodge

As if I've been facing the sea
Framed by a wooden sill

He set down his knapsack by the bed
Opened it to retrieve his pajamas
A comb, a towel, and a toothbrush

Knowing he'd be sleepless tonight
He took out a pen, placed it on the drawer
And set his notepad next to it

Perhaps he would write a few words
Knowing he'd be sleepless tonight

Just stop working already
—Also, the sea isn't sleeping

Once they'd experienced the sea
Together on the beach
They played volleyball, chased each other
Watched the sunset

Today he just wanted to look at the sea
Just like that
By himself

"The group I'm leading
Will lodge in my heart tonight."

He muttered to the owner of the
Lodge

3. My Name

How many of you are there?
Our whole family is here

Only you?
Why, this owner of the lodge
Lacks a sense of humor—

The times have trained us into
A nomadic nation
Always lugging our possessions

The journey from one village to the next
Is completed on the computer

I left my computer at home
I fled from my computer

Those who follow
Scatter midway
All the grieving, happiness
Leave piece by piece

In front of your lodge
I've become an estranged other

Everything starts again
You're the owner of the lodge
What's your name

The Sea is my name

4. I Couldn't Tell You Apart

I was waiting for you to walk
Through the door
To plant a kiss on you

Your arm, mobile
Catches my waist
Now aren't we a big clan

Locked inside the map
Some stain
Rites and customs belong to the female
Waiting for a god to fulfill

Then he leaves, feet driving the waves
For another stain
Sporting an accent and a dialect

The coastal rocks are imposing
You say, those are his parting gifts

I look at the photo, and find
You and he are
Identical twins

When you kiss me
I couldn't tell you both apart

5. Degeneration

Sea, I pronounce you king, pronounce you queen,
Pronounce you imperial bodyguard over my former territories

The waves retreating day by day look like
My wedding dress, my ceremonial robes
My swaddling clothes, my shroud

Overthrown one by one—rushing forward, yet
Dismissed from office. An age-old proposition
In the sea—all the former days
Amount to nothing

(—Time doesn't operate there—)

—He's colossal, my imperial edict
For forty days and nights, he suffers thunderstorms, as well as drought, cast by the Dark Lady of the Nine Heavens
Back in the cycle, he degenerates to earth
Words now illegible—

6. Rocks

It's like that each day—
My eyes and ears
On long strolls

A street
Strings along dusk and mist
Toward the shore

Oh, those young ones—
The rocks finally
Settle down

I, nearing from the other
Side, can't shake off this old baggage

(—The seawater laps against it daily
A tumultuous inside)

He said they would carve
A cross-shaped
Hourglass

Such that the rocks
Hid their practice deeper within

Only upon staying longer
Would you realize
He always said thus

7. Other provinces

Other provinces don't exist here
Here other provinces are the sea

They say that's the hinterland
That's the river flowing through the hinterland

Meandering, tumbling along, aimed at
The sea's direction

The wave crest's bitterness and joy
Whirlpooled
Then sank in the water

Time and again
Exhibiting in the sky
Some life's turmoil

(—Is it possible
For us to thaw
In more broad-mindedness)

Yet my eyes
And the shifting focus of my eyes

—Those waves and waves
Resist and embrace each other

8. Sail

All discarded rivers run upstream in time
Collecting here

All newborn rivers perk up their small arms
Their pure white mouths

Also, those annexed, dispersed
Severed, and judged
Are all resurrected today

I'll stand here in long repose
Watch the spectacle of multiple rivers gushing forth

About the sea, which has been thus defined
Made scientific, treated as a specialty
At the end, it's known only impotently
By one name

I recovered my previous set of eyes
Those legs
Delivered by one minor stream
To the coast with an abundant plot

Let me tell you
(—I'll tell you in a careless
text)

I'll settle down here

My sail
(—light as a goose feather)
Will be hoisted

9. Let's Make Up

Midway in my travel
Grotesque rocks jag out of my body

Scatter along the coast
Non-stop

Before those neat dark clouds come over
I'd better reach the harbor

—I've just resurrected
And merged with the sea

I reckon I've said
Words they don't know

—Let's make up

I've heard last night
Words said to you
In the hotel ten minutes away

I said I'd like to add you
As a line in the scriptures

A line of oracle bone script
Among my scriptures

Neither requiring time to decode—
Nor the hard work of an archaeological team—

I put you on the coast
Where dusk walks each day

Together with a few white birds
Using my hands, their beaks or wings
To caress or carve

New oracle bone script
—Our shared practice

Daughters

Daughter W

Oh, some of these daughters
Invented waves of the twentieth century

Their swimming postures are unique
Some foam at the mouth, some angle their feet to the sky
      But they don't die
In the dauntlessly crashing waves

The sea, vast enough to cradle their heads and another
   Makes them grow into islands
   And elongate some continents

Nature   sends its messengers
Sets these daughters' deeds adrift

The waves carry these daughters, those
   Like the moon or the sun
Into the twenty-first century

              Farther away

Daughter F—grieving over M

She bends her waist, reclines above the sea
Nothing of pleasure to wake her up

   (A formidable body like hers drifting on the sea)

Sails of the wind, like curtains on the threshold
Isolate the world and bear tidings

   When the world slopes
It releases the call of birds, as well as human scent
And the June song of cicadas
   On Sunday   the bell sounds out on time
From the cross-affixed church

She would cough and sneeze, sea water would
   Seep out from the corner of her eyes
Her body, still arched like a bow and arrow
Becomes a little taut

   (A formidable body like hers drifting on the sea)

They said, this is the Pacific Ocean   (but where's the peace)
This is the Black Sea   (but here you can't tell black from white)
This is the Dead Sea   (yet she's still alive)

She didn't die. But humans buried her
Using her arched body
Using the gray garb of seawater

Nothing of pleasure to wake her up

Daughter R

Here's where I settle down, get on with work
Why am I not aware of this

This wok spatula
This bookshelf   this writing desk
    This room of my own
Powder magazine   munitions factory

Entering the new century of the twenty-first
    Way to warfare

That's all there is to what we've accomplished

Daughter H

We as daughters should just zip our mouths
Let the men deal with it

You warned me repeatedly, taught me
With such an admonition

Others admire your marriage
You have everything from a house, a car, to a son

Still why are you depressed
The doctor said (he's a dude)
At night when you can't sleep when you are dizzy
    In the ears   your intermittent
Headache strikes   frequently

Not knowing the cause, I let him treat me

(he's a dude)
The doctor said

I've prescribed the highest dose
You don't require anything else but the sea

Daughter X

I recite the Diamond Sutra by the sea
Develop a mind that abides in nothing

I recite this to her   (to transfer merit they said)

Defeated by men, she was bedridden for three
Or thirty years
              (But the men were masked
        Standing by her bed)

Changed nurses seven times, but

She could still invent illnesses worth a lifetime—
    Diabetes, hypertension, depression, upper respiratory infection
    Fracture, bedsore, myasthenia, cataract
The doctor carted out his props—
    Feeding tube, catheter, oxygen tank, syringe
              Intubation, tracheotomy

She was saved again and again, decorated
    Like a warrior in outer space
    Her mouth zipped shut, with just one eye open

Don't feel like seeing clearly? I said
I want to bring you   (to see the sea)
By the sea
You can breathe your last breath

But as a woman, I have zipped my mouth shut
    (You taught me well)

I can only make use of the Diamond Sutra
        (They don't know what I'm talking about)
To produce a tacit understanding
    This secret Way   most deeply subtle

Daughter S

"I tie a few knots in the mosquito net
        And hang it before I sleep."

Why is sleeping so troublesome
After the mosquito net, I must lock
        three successive doors, then
    Block them with chairs

All this for being ill at ease
Ill at ease in this world

The god you summon hasn't arrived
It's in your mind, they'd say

You conjured illusory things

To make them real

Since he's both real and illusory
He would not appear

All things stem from the mind
Put in some effort there, they'd say

Hence you read for a long time by the sea
Walked for a while, and thought
    The sea and your mind were the same

Let them laugh who will   or not
It's a dialectic

Daughter M

The house we built together you and I
Is already destroyed

Its corners are leaking
Its walls are collapsing

There's no electric supply
There's damaged glass

The remnant furniture   kitchen utensils
Are discarded on the floor

We've no strength to rebuild
Another house

I can only build up myself on my own to be alone
I can only build up, by myself, a foreign land somewhere else

But you—you've already built up your own foreign land
   In the hospital with new, original equipment
On your bed you've built up
A room of your own

Daughter T

You supported me by the arm   the other daughter
We walked in the company of men, zigzagging, limping
They only left us such a crack

Sometimes we were overtaken and blocked
Loudly threatened by them   at one point we really
                     Flinched
We flagged down a taxi
Managed to break through the siege

But they sent us to the local police station
Two men greeted us. They were debating

So can we leave now
You are both banished

So long then
To freedom

Daughter L

Why did they treat you like this
   Because you're a daughter

You still recall the harassment into the night the
Assault in childhood you thought was a dream was a
Nightmare lacking experience you recall those shadows

You were both scrawling a multi-colored happy family but that
Black you finally used to outline the edges of the whole portrait
Made it complete and so then black became your color they'd
   Say that's style

Because you're a daughter you formed your style from the twentieth
   century
Until the twenty-first daughters started to form their style because you
Produced the black the black came out black smelted from the deepest
(or even deeper)   layers of the sea

   As style

Daughter K

We thought they would speak on your behalf

Stop wishing
They occasionally play the role of woman

We must learn to use our own words eventually

Practice bit by bit
Speak

Like a baby babbling
Broken, fractured, muddled
    Incomprehensible
Why not

We ought to listen to our

Treasure, silently, come here to the sea
To use the sea's mosquito net
The sea's pillow. Its bedding

Silently
Listen to the sea's cradle song
Sweetly
Being fed to you

II

And Then Later

A dark stairway. How I liked
That dark. Stairway. Leading to Dadaocheng's
Bustling mansion

Banquet tables filled the ground floor. A floor above we
Ran between the hallway columns, fussed over
The guests, bringing joy and a prosperous air

Servants shuttled back and forth, serving hot dishes, tangyuan, dessert
And exquisite food rarely seen—
It wasn't even a wedding. But post-war peace
Must have made us chill. Ready to celebrate
Any red-letter day, or when frat groups take turns
To host. Children paid these details no mind

Not knowing (what) war (meant). (What) exchanging toasts (meant)
(What) red-letter days (meant). Only happiness. Happy that so many
Showed up to put on this great show. Rigged out in their best. Suitably
Mannered. With bottomless booze. The kitchen producing endless food

We enjoyed. Escaping from the adults' stern voices, and running
    upstairs
To survey the din below, then running around the galleries, before going
To the third floor. There we stopped.
We saw that dark stairway.
Its darkness bristling with more excitement—

Mother and great-aunt, along with silly aunt, sitting
On the dark steps. Speaking softly
Great-aunt then started crying, while silly aunt laughed rashly. We
Then fell silent. Sat there in stealth. Not letting mother see us
We pretended to tiptoe away, bounced back downstairs. One of us let out a laugh
We then played catch around the banquet tables. Quickly forgetting that dark stairway

Soon after, mother and great-aunt came through with
Fresh make-up, with red flowers in their hair, decked out in pearl necklaces
Smiling rapturously. The whole audience smiled rapturously

And then later, who would remain in that dark stairway

My Mother who is a Centenarian

Why don't you eat?
She stays silent

Why don't you talk?
She smiles faintly

Why do you only smile?
She moves her mouth

I say, *are you okay?*
She opens her mouth suddenly

I see a dark opening in the
Hole, its teeth withered
And scattered, its tongue gnawed
blood-stained, somehow

Before I faint
I seem to hear my mother who is a centenarian
Say, *I've lived too long!*

Then I think I hear a laugh
Resembling a sob
Reaching into a distance

A gold-rushed city

Swap

She can no longer stomach the
Food I give her

She's got to stomach medicine
And those she doesn't love

Hence her soul has changed
Into someone she detests

This is when I learn about
the body

The deep blue of sunset
The gray clouds blooming against the sky
Too, bear relation to our bodies

The unavoidable shudder
Thunder and lightning
Too, bear relation to our bodies

All the bodies
In this world are stacked against each other
Gnawing, digesting, loving, and not loving
I am yours. You mine
We exchange our intestines. Our hearts. Even
What we call hate

Please know
That time's an issue
—I've often neglected this

Time
Will manage to swap back
All things

White

No longer bedridden
It seems, she becomes a lady in white
Scanning the room

She sees herself wearing a hospital gown
Intubated through her nose
Sporting a catheter

Six meals a day
100cc per meal

Turned every two hours in bed
But the helper forgets sometimes—having
Dozed off

The bruises on her butt
Split open as bedsores

She wants to speak
But she turns white—
Circling the room, she searches and indeed finds
Someone to speak on her behalf

By her bedside
Just a bit further
—beyond the afternoon sunlight

On the short, dark cabinet
There's an alarm clock
A photo frame

She falls inside
Breaks into a youthful smile
Befitting the ages of thirty-eight or nine

That summer she was wearing
A well-fitted white dress
She'd styled her hair
(—that hair scent lingers)

She and her lover went on a trip

All Her Life

During the first half
Surrounded by things she loves

Her sons   husband   bank savings   the house
   a golden necklace
A pretty hat   an imported Japanese dress

During the second half
Surrounded by things she doesn't love

Her sons   husband   bank savings   the house
   a golden necklace
A pretty hat   an imported Japanese dress
Her daughter-in-law   the wheelchair   the helper
   depression   lack of appetite difficulty speaking   bedsores

Without Hope

She lies in bed without hope
I ride on the bus for two hours
To see her
And help tidy her up

Prop her head up
Massage its acupoints
On her temples and crown
These are important points

Massage her neck and back
Containing governor and conception vessels
In charge of blood circulation

And her spinal column
Fueling her posture

In front, where the heart is
Requires gentle pressure
To pass on warmth

Next, after massaging her hands
I interlace our fingers
To perform hand-lifting exercises

Letting her know
There's another hand in this world
To help her

And then, to get rid of bedsores
Those scars
Bearing marks—
They'll spread
Without early treatment

Never mind, let's get rid of them—
Don't get stuck on a tough spot

Pat her legs up and down
To strengthen their muscles
Sending her energy

Though lying in bed without hope
She is slightly changed
Pearls form slowly
From her eyes

I am slightly changed too
My body feels warm
Pearls on my body appear on every pore

Freeze

Red light, green light
My youth and I
Played this game

Red light, green light
My mother—she and I play
She lies in bed

Wati and I help her sit up
Lie down, turn in bed

She does not reply
Our words
Nor does she nod or shake her head

Luckily her eyes can move, turn to me
Red light, green light
This game has made a comeback
My youth and I

Sew

Sew a piece of clothing for my mother
I would like to cover this body
Sew a body for my mother
I would like to cover this heart
Sew a heart for my mother
I would like you to stay

How Come My

Doctor
How come my tears don't flow out
But only inside

My throat is clear
But I don't feel like speaking

Often, I think of the ancient cave
That dim flame
Shining on one's face

The cave is warm
Dark
Humans coil up like animals

A morsel
Soothes her empty stomach

Aging she goes alone
To snowstorm's cliffs

Like snow
She seeps into the soil

Why do I always think of that tree
At snowstorm's edges

Is it because of my body
That she is nourished

Is humans' final resting place
The hospital bed
Or one's own bedroom

Why do I always think of
Père David's deer in the woods
Their green eyes gazing at me
Four in total

Slowly leaping over my body
Vanishing into the darkening
Jungle, I glimpse the beauty
Of its last jump

Doctor, where does it go
Why do I always want to know

A Christening

They gave our organs
Several names

Lungs during peaceful times
Exhaustion during times of war

During peaceful times they are
Heart   liver   intestines   stomach
During times of war they are
Embolism   sclerosis   canker   infection   abscess

Our bodies resemble
A city wall and moat

When the enemies come
The chain bridge across the moat
Come up and down freely   guarding the throne
And his favored concubines, courtiers, and guards

The essential area of kingly environs
Still saw the king's power freely operate

Yet these historians
Must get to the bottom of
A dynasty's collapse

Perhaps a close attendant allied with some minister
Or the court physician used a nostrum

Or perhaps a favored concubine allied with her brothers
And pricked him with a witch's curse

Or he became decrepit and dizzy himself
Missing out on state affairs, whereupon those around him
Borrowed his imperial brush

Anyhow, very few die from
A catastrophic battle of the century directed by himself
Or on a lonely battlefield where mortal bodies come to blows

(—He doesn't know, loneliness is—
A battlefield with no enemies)

What this ought to be called
Is missing from their pages

Language
for M

Me and you—two
   Orphans

The smile of two generations
   Is shattered

You guard the cross-shaped window frame
I walk out of the door

We meet our lot in life—
That assassin wrapped in a face shawl
A short knife waiting in ambush

You lie on the bed
Unable to speak

In the seaside gone into hiding
I changed my name
At the refugee's abode
I regain my language

That must be—
A gradually dimming star atlas—
Gazing out from the window
Or by the sea

An irrevocably lost
Each other

Photograph

Sitting there the three women
Had a rare meeting, now on the dining room sofa
I wanted to take their photo

"I won't die." She just took a leave of absence from the sanatorium
And her two sons drove to pick her up

Did you eat well? No.
How many to a room? Five.
"I can't speak anymore. See, my teeth are gone."

I want her to open her mouth.
"My teeth have fallen out, so I cannot speak."
I want her to open her mouth.
There are two rows of false teeth.

"I haven't slept in thirty years."
It's awful. Really awful.
"Maybe I won't die."

This time she cut her hair short
Her right eye looks strange, having shrunk
The helper took her from my elder brother's house
What did you eat this morning? Porridge.
Porridge is easy to digest, why can't you finish it?
"She slept after eating." Wati added

Do you recognize me? She nods
What about Mingzong? She nods
What about Chengzong? She nods

I give her a massage.
Starting from the head. First the temples
The ears	then down to the shoulders	armpits
Vertebrae	buttocks	legs	feet
Are you comfortable? She nods

Soon she looks pensive, her lips look
As if she's been on a lonely celestial body
A thousand million eight thousand *li* from earth

My younger sister's husband brought her over
With an S-shaped vertebrae, he's much shorter than before
Is your headache gone? Very much so.
What about now? Now my ears ache.
How are your ears? I feel like I have three of them.
I hear alright in one, but it's loud in the other, and soft in the third.
How's your sleep? Quite bad. The heavy prescription doesn't even help.

The three women sit there
I want to take a photo of them

The three women sit there stiffly
So does their combined age of two hundred

Like three celestial bodies
Hit by meteors

So we stopped talking
And took a photo

Just the Same

My elder sister's at the hospital
Lying down in the same posture
As mother

I caress her hair
Her palms, her arms, her chest
As if I'm caressing two bodies

I ask if she's feeling better today
Or the same

The same, without a response

The same look, the same
Skeletal frames, the same nasogastric tube
Syringes at the back of her hands

Just the same, my muttering keeps muttering
Like a storyteller memorizing
The skeletons of a story, muttering just to
Dispel the silence

(Most likely
It's profound within—)

I leave the hospital, just the same
I feel a surge of emotions, just the same
I question the Creator—I just had to
Keep questioning, keep talking to her
Just the same, my tears flow
—Just the same, without a response

I cry, just the same, feeling spooked
I reach home, return to write daily, just the same
Writing, just the same, without a response

(Most likely
It's profound within—)

A House of a Kind

Mother appears in my room, saying
My bones are broken, you've got to get me a wheelchair
And a helper

My brothers occupy the living room and go at each other
Soon they make a show of wrists and legs and their wives
Cheer them on and eyeball one another

My elder sister sits on the sofa, muttering I am
A robot who does not eat, drink, or die, and I
Want you to give me money

My younger sister covers her head in agony, saying that sand is in her ears
Worried that her children can't hear her calling out

On the phone, B said I cut off a breast and my uterus
And need to keep up with chemotherapy while T's email said she dreamt that her dead
Dad couldn't find the way to hell and so returned home panic-stricken

My nephew was barbequing downstairs he grilled five hundred sticks of mutton in a day three hundred sticks
Of pork six hundred sticks of beef while his mouth kept grilling five thousand sticks of welcome

Customers surge at him in waves surge at the door and the street corner
Their hands burning their legs roasting their mouths grilling they keep saying BBQ
BBQ is the only reason to live

This house is built bigger and bigger, I pass through a high-rise condo
And hop onto a train at the intersection
The train is grilling and grilling rapidly each house it passes by

I love you all, I tell the people behind me, but I must get in front
There's a house in front of the front of the (grilling—)
Train

New and Old

"I've got new siblings."
"Why are your tears flowing."
"You'll ask my old siblings."
"Why are your tears flowing again."
"My tears are old siblings, as well as my new ones.
Able to answer all questions."

Isn't That

Doctor, there's water in my stomach
Like ocean waves crashing against my stomach walls
Reaching upward, along my windpipe, esophagus, and turning right
At my throat's crossroads, finally reaching my ears with a roar like beating drums

"That's not water, it's your tears—"

The tears in my stomach formed a gigantic population
From waking up in the morning, to going to the bathroom, restaurants, and leaving the house
To passing through the intersection
They follow me, turning right, into my childhood, until they pass the lane of my youth
The main road of my adulthood, finally reaching my right ear with a roar

"That's not your tears, it's your fear—"

The fear in my stomach agitates me daily, becoming a tenacious cell
Part of my genes
My fear and I look at the mirror, we place it in a pot and water it
Feed it brown rice, meat, and juice
Wrestle with it, be sullen and troubled by it, we seem to share lots of
Happy times

"You've got to embrace the fear—"

Doctor, I haven't grasped its appearance
I run non-stop from my stomach to other organs and rest there
Before running elsewhere
I feel lost all the time, losing my relatives, friends, and body
The gap between my organs widens, my fear occupies a larger space
I've searched for Buddha, Jesus, Krishnamurti, Jane Roberts
But they stopped in my head without entering my stomach
There's still roaring in my ears

"Don't fight it, embrace the fear—"

Yes, Doctor—my life, I get it, is only about fear, that's the proof
Of my existence. Yes, Doctor
I step closer, try to get close to it
That will empower me—
I can't ever lose it again.

Hereafter

Might I remind you
After forty years of age, a year flies by like a month
Suddenly you're fifty

After fifty, a year flies by like a day
Suddenly you're sixty

After sixty—
I know you still don't understand life

But seventy comes
And you and your siblings are naughty
You're forced to drink tea, coffee, play cards
Practice Buddhism, stay healthy, or do volunteer work
You join tour groups again and become grandriders
But you still don't understand life

After eighty, you grow up dramatically
You age, you get that
This is life

What Each Family Has

Each family has a sick person, a murderer, a bully,
An angel, a prophet

One of each, perhaps three
Or maybe a third of each
It depends on how honestly they look into it

In an introspective moment
Each person brags that they are an angel, a prophet
But the angel's wings become a stick
The stick becomes a knife
The knife becomes a prophet
The whole family will start to act differently

In a traditional family
This enclosed system
Recalls a textbook with a VCD
Vivid and thought-provoking

A small family today, according to
The law of conservation of mass
Still contains those roles
But in an abstract sense

If we isolated each person
And sampled them
Things get more enigmatic

Even with the help of X-ray, MRI,
Ultrasound, ECG,
It's still hard to differentiate
Which part is angel or prophet, which
Of him is a murderer, a bully

And what's more he is outfitted with
Appendages like a phone, iPhone, iPad
Combined at random, allocated at will
Accruing good karma, multifarious evildoing

—Unmatched even by the ancients, who would consecrate him as a god
Or dismiss him as a cock-and-bull story

He can't be sampled from a traditional human family
Nor imagined within textbooks of human history
Via self-combination, he created the new human
—Invincible, eternally changing

All traditional human families
Please beware

Alms Bowl

In the morning, I bring in my poem, scoff down three bowls of rice
At night, I put in my phlegm, cough, bathwater, depression

Here's what separates me and M
She accepts what's bequeathed across generations, receives the alms bowl
And swallows its bitter contents

In a special corner at home (—the altar)
Being respectful, on guard

I've taken possession of half, at most
—Plus, I use a different alms bowl
And I misbehave

I walk out with that alms bowl. Without awaiting orders
I'm on my way

Oh, the trip to the gray temple
Is long and lonely
—I've just got to revel in
The words I've concocted

And wait for me to put on other colors

Talking to Prisoners

I've mastered a technique
To talk to prisoners

I pierce through walls
To find the one person
Trapped in bed

I will use a beam of light
To type words on his heart

Black background white font
A5
PMingLiU 12pt font

The second Sunday in May
The third Sunday in June
Or other ritual-bearing holidays

I will put my technique to the test
Develop a child's
Endless potential

Because of this I become a child
And get my reward

"You create your own reality"
Painstakingly I write this
Page by page as an exercise

My master once put in such an effort
And shot his beam at me
Through the walls—

You saw the crack
A case in point

Dreams

My form contains them—
My parents, grandparents, great-grandparents
Now I can't locate them

Australia, the Americas, Africa, Iraq, or Madagascar

Following the universe's plans, their forms change,
Throw off the past, and become unrecognizable

Yet my form contains them—
(—What I know of them)
Becomes clearer, multitudinous

Add or multiply a memory
You get a colossal memory cluster
Which connects and crisscrosses, warns and calls us
Without halting

Taking another form in another place
They occasionally stir in my memory, and send me messages
In my dreams
—Brushing past, exchanging no words, or recalling nothing when
   I wake

This law of the universe—

My fate—
Has to dream constantly
From now to eternity—

III

Z and Me

"At a faraway place there lies Z"
—from Borges, Preface to *A History of Eternity*

Midway

Midway in life, I meet that person
We walk and talk, leaping past the wilderness and another city
Take a bus through several small towns, mountains, to a faraway place

We buy some daily supplies, rent a house to rest
Buy farm-fresh produce in the morning, do odd jobs in the afternoon, and sleep early

I think of Z suddenly one day

I left without saying goodbye, of course Z felt really bummed
That hurt naturally came from our daily discussions of literature and art
The classics and ink stones on the desk
And our edifying banter

I left without saying goodbye, plunging him into depression, or did he
Hold on, as before, to what we loved
Thinking of Z made me cry a lot

Today I go on the road knowing I can't find Z
But I wish to say to him—

Thirty Years

I haven't seen Z in thirty years

When I moved out
He moved out from another there
We didn't know where we'd relocated to

Not meeting was intentional
Having lost our coordinates
We could still enjoy our days

That said we ran into each other
On a less crowded train
Somehow, I managed to tug my pants back on

He wasn't taken aback by his sudden appearance
Neither was I

Another person and I
Walk in a winding alley

Seeing him reappear in the winding alley's
Most winding spot

In front of a dark house
He stood
As if to say this is my house

I just looked
Without stopping

Without startling my companion
Without startling anyone

He knows
I know

After thirty years
I start to have
Such dreams

Cactus

It was I who kissed you

It was I who (took the lead and diligently)
Kissed your dark

Hometown and brown soles of
Your cactus

My chest cavity hides atlases
Water, nutrients. When happy
It blooms

Toward the desert, in the countryside
I smile and speak softly
Talk about literature, faith, and love

And my thorns (—my flesh bearing crosses)
Soften—I'm not a powerful courtier
Of this earth—I am summoning

The person who kissed me

Note: I forgot that I wrote this a while ago!

In February 2015, Hsi Muren (Xi Murong) sent me a self-made card, and wrote, "Here are some newspaper clippings from a while back," and affixed this poem. Her handwriting looked sincere and energetic, making this poem interesting to look at. Suddenly I recalled that this poem was published way back in *United Daily News*'s literary supplement, but I've yet to publish it in a poetry collection. My first thought was to embed this poem in the series, given the dejection and joy of a serendipitous reunion.

Civilized

Does such a celestial body exist
What's mine is safely in your orbit

So is your star, safely in my
Orbit—

Rotating thus
We illuminate the other
And spot each other's light
Despite bad weather

We are not afraid come
Extraordinary times

We've been through so many tough times
From Genesis to the Book of Revelation
From the Vimalakirti Sutra to the Heart Sutra
In Nineveh's imperial library
You've engraved a clay tablet version
Of the Flood, Noah's ark, the Garden of Eden

But here I respond with
The Creator goddess Nüwa, the founder of the Xia dynasty Yu the
    Great, and his father Gun
Oracle bone script, bronze ware, and chimes

Separately we got tattoos
Separately we adorned planets

Yet we could make out
The civilization we've developed on our own

Such feelings and rational thinking—
Disparate elements—

Half

At my age, half of me
Has already become the West

Yet I know, there's someone in the West—
Whose half has become the East

Looking out from my room onto the small street
With a leafy canopy and luxuriant foliage

We walk together and discuss
The history of the earth—
My deepest memory is of those works
—making us embark on a perilous journey

After putting on drag, and before
Lifting into other galaxies
Resplendent, twinkling, we are mere
Light and shadow

Pursuing our fixed stars—

That Celestial Body

Z, we've known each other before the School of Athens was built
Fennel branches in the dark, set aflame
(—Fire had just been invented)

Thanks to our curiosity for a celestial body
In the late night's cool breeze
We saw each other's shadows

We tried to find out
About an earlier birthplace of humans
And whether feelings spur rational thinking
Or vice versa

But then we put in words:
"That celestial body shifts ever so slightly—"

—Almost the height of a mountain
Where dust absconds
We'd like to know

When we say (—on the ground) how
To build a beautiful country
We gaze downward to find weak fennel branches
Stirring, ready to burst out in sparks

That made us stop talking for a time

Cross-examination

Oh, Z, we get it
Why we're strong doesn't
Come from the people and land

But from the void—

Those lofts, or mythical lands on Kunlun
Those letters penned in blood on eternal nights, those verses sewn
   into clothes

Those divination practices—the ocean's depth, or
The universe's expanse

Having found that most erudite priest in Nineveh
And asking him about the life and death of Earth
Its various beginnings and ends

We have come to love this cross-examination

Myth

I often review such a scenario:
I walk alone on this world
Just as it is being created

I am the first human
Without fear and needs

Upon meeting you
I develop my five senses
Eyes, ears, nose, tongue, and my body splits

Relatives and friends come from
God knows where. I'm hustled away. Sometimes tossed into the air
Sometimes coiling on the ground

Then I'll notice another you
Becoming another person, your body robust
Holding up the universe, asking me if
I remember the Creation

Really, that was a lovely time
I know, it's not a myth

Language

Dear Z, after all this, I still can't
Say that I love you
I've rehearsed *dear* forever

While in exile
Language is so subtle that it hurts

Some words are like aloof passersby
Grasping an umbrella to strike where it aches

How can they be
Oblivious to the inner being of words
And their negative shadows

Scurrying along, my alert self
Seems unbothered to plan for rain or shine
Humming a tune—clearly taking leave of a blessed haven
Or returning to it

How can they
Bustle about an ordinary street
Becoming a crowd

Using those words I know so well
Works out, helping me live well

Dreaming and Waking

Z, I have four cabinets in my dream
I open them, but they are not mine

One of them
Has a terrarium

I'd like to destroy it
Secretly transplant its contents
To the wild

—The wilderness is out there
I quickly thought it over
If there was a place out of sight
But failed

This home belongs to two others
I and another other
Engage in small talk

I wish to tell him
The ins and outs
Of my love-hate relationship with the others
But failed

—Someone here is
Thwarting my plan

Aggrieved and angry
Until I wake up
Aggrieved and angry
Who they are escapes me

Betrayal

Besides death
Nothing can keep us apart

What about betrayal
Just once

If that's the case
We don't need to separate

What about twice
Twice betraying you
—We don't need to separate

What about thrice four times
What about five or six times

What about thrice four times
Five or six times
(—That form of betrayal isn't death)
We don't need to separate

What about seven eight nine or ten times
Dear Z, I often imagine
Such a sacred conversation

Such that often—my eyes
Are filled with difficult tears

Cracks

On the vase we molded together
There's now a small crack

Visitors
Taking off their shoes by the door
Would say, what a pity, this vase

Entering the room, sitting on the rattan chair
They would start reminiscing about our times
Comfortably sip tea

As if all young people knew no cracks
Able to withstand such chatter and remodeling

We redecorated the vase
Covering it with longer sprigs
Or using plain designs and colors
Against its corners

Probably it was you who said:
"Remember when we first saw this vase—"

Stop bringing it up, I reply to myself:
I only want to arrange the sprigs
Replace them daily
Either shop for them
Or pluck them from our little garden
That's all I could do

The Other Side

During exile
She got tense at ignorant children's noises
The old neighbor's cough, day and night
Reminding her to no end, that some pursuit
Is closing in or slacking
Affecting her night's vertebrae

She's escaped twice to another street
Another building, and from the rooftop
She gazes often
At her life on the other side

She sees the girl who emerges from noisy obstacles
To compete in a match

She sees in alleys and towns
What exactly she is circling around

Her exercise is intense—
Pas de deux, diving, rock climbing, Ferris wheel

She performs crying, cursing, despairing, thumping
She performs magic, her body being opened and closed

Finding her soul
—Death has made its debut
Gorgeously present

She's received gifts, tender moments
Have anointed her
But the karma of exile—
There's always a family, an organization, or a country
Standing right in front of her

During exile, she muses: I can play
Between this rooftop and that
One, I can
Prop up a steel wire

Rooftop

From the rooftop you'll get to
Glimpse the past, shuttling about in alleyways

Glimpse danger and sorrow
I'd like to prevent

But no. Even recollecting
Is timid for me

I saw a giant creature swallowing her, later
She reappeared on another street

I couldn't prevent it—it's she
Who spurred me on

—It's she who made me stand on the rooftop
Fussing over how myriad changes
Occur

Two Lamps

Always I get to see your body's two lamps
Always I get to see their brilliance and dimming
Even their dying out

You secretly walk past me
Always I get to know the past
These ten years, twenty years, your life, how
To extinguish the lamps

We speak in hushed voices
That sometimes mimic ritual forms
We both ponder this: the past is better
The past is better

In the flickering light
We see each other
Being smiled at, as heightened tones twist
Shine upon us

Yet dormant moments reveal
Our distress, as we both gaze into
The extinguishing flame

—Jet-black
Ruins of war

We both ponder this: only if you knew, only if

Olive Trees

Midway in exile…
Z, you're one of the reasons why I stay behind

My shoulders ache so bad
At night
—Only as I dream

I'm bearing weight that exceeds the limit
—Distorted facts and the hounding of canine teeth

Ran my seven-day itinerary into seven years

Z, the olive trees you plant
Is now an estate

The day you have me over
Your boy servants line up to greet me on verdant paths

My hiding spot is deep in your estate
A breezy area

—I'll take a rest here
Three days, or three years, thirty years

Would depend on whether
The tree is canopied for eternity

The Years

Z, I recognize the scar on your lower leg
I recognize that bed
I recognize father's orchard

I've shot down our formidable enemies
But one escaped
Valiantly he led away all his companions
—Such were the years of resurrection
And relentless attacks on me

I'm flanked by peacekeepers
Who convince me to forget
Enjoy much or have nothing
Move forward or back up

Along this winding corridor, Chinese-style
I'll linger for a bit

Not tired, merely pausing
Deep in thought, replacing rest—

Banishment

Why treat me like this
Four-faced cherub
Sword with rotating flames

—I won't go back there again

I will die and die again
Death's flavor escapes you

While dying
I can be reborn anytime

How to come alive escapes you
—I answer only to myself

You won't lose your temper again, you said
Nor destroy me with the flood

You're nasty—
You use self-destruction
To end me

Midway I keep warning the other me
But the duplicate cherub
The duplicate sword with rotating flames
The duplicate wrath of God
Appear

I can't control that the other me
Duplicated God's country
Even God's duplication is complete

I'm banished, once again
Banished—

I won't go back there again

Pay no Mind

Z, I'm paying you no mind
Just as you did me earlier

When I come from the east, you've set up a roadblock there
When I come from the west, you've laid down a trap there

I've played up my homesickness
Collected innumerable bugs
To gnaw at my heart

To turn day into night
Night into darker night

Z, I wear my old uniform
To act rich for everyone

Back where I live, I burn
The classics, one by one

Sometimes I singe my hair
My eyebrows, they say
I'm prettier that way

It's their warning
—Losing you is like losing the world

Those are their words
What about losing me

How to put it, being ordinary
I chanced upon your strapping self
Espying you, I clung onto your tall scepter

Hence, I've got to lose you
For my world to be mine

Note: The first two lines are adapted from Eileen Chang's letter to Hu Lancheng: "I'm no longer fond of you, whereas you've stopped liking me earlier."

Hide and Seek

I've become
That bystander

—He finds this person interesting

I wear a shawl for the cold
He asks why
And rubs the burning edge of my shawl

I heat up my bitter gourd and vegetables in a take-away box
He asks why
And comes over to see the shabby greens

I think about the two brothers
But won't recount their story

I look at the garden's flower bunches
Glistening from the rain

Their drops are slowly quelled
Becoming a bystander's good mood

I won't recount
The story of my exile

As for the demise of my royal family and city
And the scattering of my kingdom

I've kept for myself
A formidable loneliness
To play hide and seek with

Cut to Shreds

Who invented such motions
Notices, ceremony, rules, order

—It was us lousy plebeians
Who designed the stage for the mediocre
Country, organization, cliques

We've always favored the mediocre
Constantly bowing, giving way
Making ourselves approachable

Those who don't know their place, or can't stand it
Flee in panic, we predict that
He'll be stranded midway, murdered
Or reduced to mediocrity

—Only this way will he not be
Cut to shreds by loneliness

Being cut to shreds is said to be the most violent
Form of corporal punishment

It's said that their howls
Have won over death

There are some who don't howl, supposedly
He doesn't feel like winning anything
Even death

Old Age

Just as I was losing my way
I turned, then turned right a little
To find a strange little garden
Hiding in the corner

To the point of exhaustion—
Suddenly, only when you're old
You discover
And comprehend its beauty

Here, you get to see so much
So, so much—childhood
Hidden under a pergola
Luring you over

Oil lamp, firewood stove, altar
Impromptu stages, outdoor cinema
Street scenes from the fifties

You live on the third alley
The second building has a Japanese house with a courtyard

A girl meets up with you
Wearing an off-white dress
With a bowknot tied to its neck
Readying her smile for school

Her smile becomes tears on your face
She leads you by your hand—
Going in, you don't feel like leaving

But—
What other sceneries are there
When old age passes by

Thinking thus activates an energy
Propelling the feet

Tears stream profusely, let them be

Teardrops

I told that running child to hold up
To ask about his childhood

His glistening eyes
Darted at me, as he walked on

A young griffon vulture
Waited at the crossroads

I felt like warning him
But it was too late, I'd woken
From my dream, I'm middle-aged

In the bathroom mirror, an elderly
Walked over and said to me
I recognize you

I sorted out my tears, classified and stored them
He said, you don't have a drawer
Why are you consuming such luxurious things

I guess I no longer respect him—
The calendar he foisted on me
Was curiously different from mine

Sound

There's a crack in that room
There I started my exile

I have parents and siblings
There I started my exile

From classrooms on Ethics and Success
I am exiled

From forty days and nights of rain
I am exiled

There's a sound that wakes you
Irregularly, like a sudden illness

You wish to sing with your real voice
But he uses his operatic one

He sprinkles perfume along the street
Captures vagrants to bathe them
Makes them listen to sutras, feeds them

I only pretend to be a wayfarer
Passing by this area, only recording
Adapting stories I glean on the road

I get it, everyone has a different libretto
You decide the sound
Of your own exile

Stagger

In my dream
You're a female Z one moment
A male Z the next

You've arrived
At my hideout city

I point out two newly constructed
Yet dated-looking buildings

We walk in step along the winding alley
Someone else escorted us like a shadow
Walking on my right side

Quietly I used another language
—Let's hurry up
That person hurried along too

—Let's slow down
That person slowed down too

We got spooked
Not knowing what to do

Since we knew not what to do
We staggered, waking from the dream

No, only I woke up—
No, it seems I was banished from it

You remained in the dream
Everything remained in the dream

Dusk

Toward the end of my exile
I went so far as to forget the bitter in life

In one's life
Washing vegetables and fruit, removing bad leaves
I went so far as to notice the taste in food

Calling me sometimes were friends
Sometimes not

I know they are their own beings
On my canvas
They are an extra stroke of colors

Yes, they'd walk in
Sit on my chair

Perhaps I would draw them
Perhaps not—

Light and shadow alternate in my studio, form and aspect change rapidly
Yet they can't compare
To the most beautiful dusk
And so, I take a walk outside

I believe dusk is why
I live—keep up with
My exercise of a spelling game

The "person" and "animal" radicals
Modular production systems like these
Sometimes bring me desolate misery

So, light and shadow dim at each sky's beating
Letting me revise some of the old days

I Like

I like watching you sitting peacefully at that spot
Drinking afternoon tea, grading homework

Yet I disrupt the Heavenly Palace, wield the golden cudgel
Busy myself with destroying everything

I like watching you bring your family around
Dining indoors, sightseeing outdoors
Forging ahead along the tracks of well-being

Yet I dash around madly, overtake, and speed race
Finish off the dragon, wrestle with humans and beasts

I like watching you build tall flats and red pavilions
In gentle, pleasant breeze, timely rain has arrived
Great scenery is within your depiction

Yet I use erotic art as the base
The ocean of desire as the frame
A wild cursive hand from a thick brush, transposing black and white
Use drawing papers that I can't cram as my game

Many years later—I ought to hurry to the end of my life
So many years later
We meet, unplanned

I like
That you ask me suddenly
Why are you by yourself

Maybe—I will ask you suddenly
Why are you also by yourself

I like
That final meeting

The Depths

Slowly I walk into the depths

Silhouette—
Swallowed up by the years
Then popping up in front, at the back

I am by myself
But also not

Some get in the way
But in fact don't

I take the winding road, far road, forked road
But I've fixed my direction

The mountain ranges rise and fall, the mist comes in waves
At dusk, I still walk
Walk slowly without stopping

You wait at the intersection
And at another you wait
For me to come to greet you

Speed, color, breed
Push us apart
And bring us together

Not surprised at all
It must be when
I'm entirely myself
That I notice you

IV

Looking at Pictures

—Utagawa Hiroshige's
Fifty-Three Stations of the Tōkaidō

1.
11th Station, Early Morning

Each detail piles up
Or scatters inch by inch
Your youthful days

The breeze that snuck into your body's crevices
The fury stationed on the apex of your heart

Some are close shots with bright colors, such as
Extinction or forging ahead, steadfastly—
Stepping toward the journey

Long shots. Often gray with fuzzy edges
Fully dipped in tears, having used up
The spare ink

Within these blurred images, the journey
Has nowhere to turn to

2.
19th Station, Crossing the River

Everyone has to cross a river
On this journey

Mules and horses bear goods, sometimes
Army supplies and gear, sometimes
Beautiful women, especially ones with bewitching makeup
They're worth measuring against gold

Sometimes manpower replaces the draught animals
The laborers take off their clothes, go naked
Bare their shoulders and necks, or their crooked heads
Their mouths crying out, their hands never idle
Their expressions many, their postures never alike

Such vivid movements—
Pulverized by life
Yet bouncing back

But the made-up women and army gear
Have only one expression
To cross the river

3.
16th Station, Boat

How to summon that boat. We're
At the crags, it's far away

As if ignorant that people on earth
Seek out companions

Two pine trees hospitably extend their arms
How many times have they summoned—

Wind, rain, sun, mountain
Everyone has labored to summon
That boat

One, two, three, four
Boats. All fates are similar

Standing upright on the sea
Pointing clearly, as if they haven't met
With the stormy seas

It's plying forward, truly—
Silent, its motion undetectable

—Neither revealing the journey's hardship
Nor caring for the occasional summon

4.
33rd Station, Three Blind Women

We are taught the journey's hardship
Three people, propping their hands on shoulders, they said we are three blind women

But we could tell
The *shamisen* strings tremor from the journey's fresh taste
—the fragrance of tree leaves, the far-flung nature of land

Their heroic tones bring succor to the weak
Their mute tones reinforce evil
But that's their fate

We are bystanders
Able to see how the journey
Takes a turn in the three strings, those bends that resonate
In mutual support

We better not name
Who
Arranged for us
To show up at the journey's most winding spot
Like envoys dispatched to perform unenviable tasks

5.
44th Station, Ishiyakushi

This nineteenth-century village has a sweet fragrance before decomposition
The year being 1832, an ordinary early winter day
The woods' leafy branches carefully patch over the thatched hut's roof
In the house, naturally, women busy about
Children, naturally, face a stern upbringing

The quiet light rays leap past three mountain ranges
Darkening the pine trees' dense leafy shade
—Darkness would be the assignment of the near future

The farmers in the rice field pile up the paddy, rush to weed before sunset
On the small road two people shoulder their luggage, trying to catch up with the horse at the intersection

The traveler riding the horse, and his two servants, stop at the gate of Ishiyakushi
Anxious, as if they've yet to find a potent medication, they start to turn left
Onto the winding path toward the shrine

They're curious to see how darkness slowly descends, how hooves
Fall without abating after they lightly touch

Rushing on the road is not darkness—
Frankly I've already known
After paying homage at the shrine, they are charged with confidence, plunging headlong
Into the twentieth century

Before darkness is shipped onto the battlefield and factories
My brush could perceive, being urged to
Stay at, this nineteenth-century village

I make do this way—
Leave the haystack's scent behind

6.
34th Station, The People on the Bridge

The twenty-first century, under renovation—
Its dignified elegance will be razed to the ground

He—a foreman
Came to earth from Heaven's court
He's orchestrating—

To convert the wooden bridge into a highway
Into a skyscraper, shopping center
A mound into a munitions factory

Today he looks afar—no, he's mourning
The people on the bridge
Going about their blessed days

One of them is Tripiṭaka, returning from his pilgrimage for the Buddhist scriptures
—This Master is readying his return to the twentieth century
The peaceful small town, his house deep in the fallow grasslands

On a sunny day he would air the sutras
Feed the white horse, dreaming that one day
He could replenish the capital's library

—This wooden bridge will disappear
He spots the widening crack

His Master Tripiṭaka is about to sink
His foot into that hole

Luckily, only dust from his shoe soles
Falls on a boat's canopy about to pass by
But no one notices

—Such a mortal life, fluttering through our times

Only that he knows
His Master Tripiṭaka
Can't live past today—

7.
14th Station, Ashes

Mount Fuji, burned into ashes by time
Looks like a reddish castle in the air

I want to proceed—

I take along my servants, horses, and female family members
I guess I was seven when I started my journey toward fading youth

My servants are elderly, my female family members include my mother
My mother's mother. The tiresome journey made them
Doze off—my loneliness is free to roam

My horse followed behind—my other servant who guides
Turning left, right, then left, right, so many turns
Of left and right, until we reach our destination

How many burnings—my face leaning left, always
Having doubts—
How many burnings until I understand
The reddish castle in the air

And learn that
The journey through the mountain is
Indeed the journey toward fading youth

8.
30th Station, For Utagawa Hiroshige

Five mountain systems, eight peaks, stretches of sand, and wooden
 bridges
Were what he saw on the journey

A small boat—two canopies, a good person
Steers from afar, about to pass through

The copse ahead—three old trees, their branches
Like stubble, forking, the other five small trees inserted between

The journey is long.
Rocks strewn on this shore. Chest and arms
Numerous flesh in disarray, about to take action
But tree leaves here have yet to sprout

Passing by, he jots down signs of life. He says
I'll let the trees germinate, let the good return home, let dreams
Be lofty, let the floodwater boldly flow

On my tiny ink slab

Epilogue

1.

Ukiyo-e is my other dimension.
Utagawa Hiroshige is another dimension.
Fifty-three Stations of the Tōkaidō is another dimension.
I prefer Hiroshige to Hokusai. Having met those who share my interest, I call them my bosom friends, like Lu Xun.
Westerners love Hokusai, wherein lies our different tastes.
Hokusai uses close-ups, while Hiroshige full-length shots.
Speaking of taste, *Fifty-three Stations of the Tōkaidō* is on my desk for me to flip through.
Gazing via full-length shots. (—One can assign the label *close-up* voluntarily)
I'm often affected by the mise-en-scène. The details of common people, when evoked, bristle with vitality.
Low rhetoric belonging to the eighteenth and nineteenth century is set free from one elegant pen.
Later generations can be traced back to coarse earlier times—while common people's coarse lives are out of the question.
The sheer term *ukiyo-e* is such a great invention.
I, too, invented my own taste of the floating world.
From Tōkaidō to the East Coast. Fifty-three stations become fifty-three poems.
I pursue this road with my full-length shot.
Long it is, life's long stretch of years.
My other dimension.

2.

Fifty-three poems, not just numbers, but nomenclatures. (—This book is not just fifty-three poems—)
My good friend—Utagawa Hiroshige from the nineteenth century is loaned for my use.
He generously let me peruse *Fifty-three Stations of the Tōkaidō*, replacing *dō* or *road* with *coast*, *station* with *poem*—its moveable-type printing can be changed freely, as we enjoy the splendor of Chinese characters.
For his generosity and inspiration, I thank him now.
All art—of course, extending to all forms of culture and technology, are grand contributions.

3.

I live on the waves. On the top of the wave, in the wave.
I lie and sleep on the east, floating here and there on a raft.
I enumerate the Milky Way, dusk, dawn, and bask in sorrow and joy.
I enumerate goodbyes, affection, dreams, and bask in sorrow and joy.
Sorrow and joy on a little boat.
By lying down quietly, I bring sunny weather, whirlpools, wind and rain.

Oblivious that it can move.
I produce, I abandon. The big sea is thus formed.
There's no opposite shore.
The opposite shore is an imaginative pretext.
I'm stating this publicly.
Writing poetry is my Temple of Apollo, my shield of Achilles.
My Sanxingdui, my Aleph.
The world is within.
I create, I live.

4.

As for the title, should it be *Fifty-three Poems of the East Coast* or *Daughters*—a title that came last minute.
I deliberated for a while.
Mother departed more than six years ago. Dedicating this book to her, I settled on *Daughters*.
I harbor deep adoration and regret toward mother.
Roland Barthes's *Mourning Diary* makes me pained whenever I pick it up.
Tears are commonplace.

—Mother's death has made me into my own mother.
I know, too, that you'll die.
Death's succession has never once changed.
Yet I forever will be a daughter in search of her mother.

5.

I preserve the three parts of *Epilogue* that I wrote earlier with *Fifty-three Poems of the East Coast* in mind.
To preserve my deep feelings for that title.
At the end, this world is made of deep feelings, what else can it be.

Translator's Afterword

A Poet's Wanderlusting Blue

LING YÜ's *Daughters* sutures three poetic sections, indicating that care work for a dying parent involves a dialogue with the self and one's favorite art. Walking through rooms of quiet banality of hospice and grief, the reader then wanders through memory scenes about Z, before ending up on the travel highway between Edo and Kyoto with the help of Utagawa Hiroshige's (1797–1858) landscape prints. What ties these tonally distinct settings and modes of looking at and visiting someone or a place, or in short, Ling Yü's way of getting involved, will be my focus.

The first and last poems tell us how to read *Daughters*. In "East Coast," Ling Yü's *blue* is inescapably geographic, a pigment sourced from nearby mythological histories. Attempting a list of "ninety-nine types of blue," the speaker trails off at "wanderlusting blue" after the patter of "Shuang-hsi blue Fulong blue Turtle Island blue Pacific Island blue Cawi' blue ukiyo blue bittersweet blue." *Ukiyo* [floating world] *blue* could refer to the "synthetic pigment" of Prussian blue linked to Hiroshige's prints, which use the "non-fugitive" dye for "better application of even shading (*bokashi*) of large sky and water areas within the landscape scene" (Uhlenbeck and Jansen 2008: 11). The gradation technique of *bokashi* applies to Ling Yü's descriptive method. Just as the printer uses wet cotton to dilute the evenly applied color's intensity (Forrer 2017: 57), Ling Yü dampens the strong inheritance of language's meaning culled from Buddhist texts and Chinese history to blend her own disappearance as an observer of life into nature's landscape.

It follows that nature's representation, not scripture, though the latter is invoked, authorizes Ling Yü's poetic reality. In this reality, Ling Yü prefers meditative, unassuming poise to dramatic, proclaiming movement. In "Epilogue," she declares her love for Hiroshige over Hokusai, whom "Westerners love, wherein lies our different tastes": Hiroshige uses "full-length shots" for the "mise-en-scène" of "common people," on which the poet can train Hokusai's tendency for "*close-up* voluntarily." Hiroshige's *Fifty-Three Stations of the Tōkaidō* (1833–34) is "another dimension" for Ling Yü, but also reflects *ut pictura poesis*: "From Tōkaidō to the East Coast. Fifty-three stations become fifty-three poems," which are "not just numbers, but nomenclatures" that "replac[e] *dō* or *road* with *coast*, *station* with *poem*." Ling Yü changed the book's title from *Fifty-three Poems of the East Coast* to *Daughters* at the last moment to express "deep adoration and regret toward mother." To view the stations, or poems, as bereavement and a "staged journey of enlightenment" puts a spin on the route's secular fame with its "link with early Buddhism in the familiar 53 stages" (Salter 2006: 66).

During the tourism boom of the Edo period (1603–1868), or new "culture of movement" (62), the *Tōkaidō* [eastern sea route] became a popular route for commoners, including women and children, to escape their mundane, laborious lives via "sight-seeing in Kyoto, pilgrimage to Ise, religiously inspired journeys to Mount Fuji and Ōyama, and trips to nearby provinces on business or for health reasons" (Oka 1982: 37). Travelers could replicate Yaji and Kita's exploits on this route from the picaresque novel (1802) using guidebooks, and Hiroshige's prints became keepsakes. The modern Ling Yü journeys through the different stations of being a daughter, or depicts the visits of multiple daughters to their mom's station of a hospital bed. In Ling Yü's juxtaposition, dying belongs to the "other dimension" of *ukiyo-e* [pictures of the floating world]:

the spiritual import of pilgrimage in death is recast in travel's light-hearted, unpredictable frivolity. In this journey, stations of health, recovery, and decay are defined by their unique settings told from different angles despite their messy schedules of arrival. Poems are scenes of domestic care, but also windows into the bedridden patient's mental state, which Ling Yü projects into East Asian tropes and visions of being on the road, not necessarily a journey into the afterlife.

Not completing the route, Hiroshige allegedly copied scenes from "available guidebooks" after the ninth station, but "reworked the line illustration" by choosing different vantage points (Forrer 2017: 53; 57). Hiroshige innovates the study of landscape when engulfed by landscape. Preferring the coast to the inland of plains and mountains, Hiroshige "designed at least around 800 prints on the Tōkaidō stations" but was "only once involved in a series of prints in the stations of the Kisokaidō" (247). Ling Yü writes on only eight stations from the most famous Tōkaidō series, upon which she bears wide-ranging *ekphrastic* interpretation: the 33rd station depicts three blind women who as "*shamisen* strings tremor from the journey's fresh taste"; at the 16th station "everyone has labored to summon / that boat"; the "traveler riding the horse" at the 44th station, having paid "homage at the shrine," "plung[es] headlong / Into the twentieth century." Every journey has unique partners, carriers, and vessels, but its destination sometimes accelerates into catastrophic time.

For example, the 34th station poem draws on the classic tale of *Journey to the West*: the scholar-monk "Tripiṭaka, returning from his pilgrimage for the Buddhist scriptures [...] is readying his return to the twentieth century," where his "house deep in the fallow grasslands" is located. But a "foreman," supposedly the monkey Sun Wukong, predicts that the monk must die to preserve the people's "blessed days." Tripiṭaka still "would air the sutras / Feed the white horse" given by the Jade Emperor. It's worth noting that Hiroshige made sketches for *Tōkaidō* as part of a shogunal entourage to deliver a white horse to the Emperor. Perhaps Ling Yü is linking Tripiṭaka to Hiroshige through a journey's worth measured in the vessel of white horses that produces commissioned art and scriptural translation to enrich the world's libraries. But destruction prevails in this series, Ling Yü propels her figures from Hiroshige's "nineteenth-century village" into the twentieth century, where "Darkness would be the assignment of the near future," or even "the twenty-first century, under renovation— / Its dignified elegance will be razed to the ground." But Hiroshige's century is apocalyptic, too: "Mount Fuji, burned into ashes by time / Looks like a reddish castle in the air." Tripiṭaka wishes to "replenish the capital's library" with the scriptures, but Ling Yü worries about the fate of more books, among other things, in the middle sequence about Z: "From Genesis to the Book of Revelation / From the Vimalakirti Sutra to the Heart Sutra / In Nineveh's imperial library."

How does the final destination of books and art relate to seascapes and hospital visits at the start of *Daughters*? After the book's first poem, "East Coast," there are two short sequences titled "The Sea is My Name" and "Daughters." In the first, a speaker observes a "he" taking a bus to a coastal lodge to write. The power to possess is vested in landscapes by humans: "Sea, I [...] Pronounce you imperial bodyguard over my former territories"; "All newborn rivers perk up their small arms / Their pure white mouths // Also, those annexed, dispersed / Severed, and judged / Are all resurrected today." But the speaker's body conforms to rugged nature: "Midway in my travel / Grotesque rocks jag out of my body // Scatter along the coast / Non-stop." The old Chinese metaphor of humans as rocks justifies the speaker's move to the sea to perfect her art: "The rocks finally / Settle down," after which the speaker writes a "new oracle bone script" with a partner, "Such that the rocks / Hid their practice deeper within." The metamorphosis of the human body into nature and then durable art is also explored in "Daughters."

So *Daughter W* begins: "Oh, some of these daughters / Invented waves of the twentieth century," which in turn make them "grow into islands / And elongate some continents" before they are borne "Into the twenty-first century." Daughters are made of seawater, but they also make waves in the Pacific Ocean, Black Sea, and Dead Sea. They carve out or turn into geological formations. By the sea, daughters write, work, heal, recite the Diamond Sutra, build a house, recall harassment in patriarchal society whose norms are propped up by the myth of a "multi-colored happy family." *Daughter L* resists:

Because you're a daughter you formed your style from the twentieth
 century
Until the twenty-first daughters started to form their style because you
Produced the black the black came out black smelted from the deepest
(or even deeper) layers of the sea

   As style

The enraged run-on line precipitates black, of ink or smelted iron—what daughters use to "form their style" from the deepest "layers of the sea." Style is Ling Yü's proposed way of mending the dissonance of personal and historical trauma across centuries—particularly the nineteenth, twentieth, and twenty-first centuries. Daughters are biological, geological, historical, or incipient mothers, though Ling Yü prefers to task daughters, instead of mothers, with the less canonical role of making *style* out of gendered tradition. It is the daughter who reimagines the mother's free travel into memory from the hospital bed. In the "Epilogue," the amphibious daughter declares, at peace, "I live on the waves. On the top of the wave, in the wave."

Overall, Ling Yü's collection is not a hermetic treatise on how waves resolve or dissolve in tradition. Books, libraries, rituals, and practices buoy *Daughters*, but the poems offload them to *stylize* the simple poetic line, like a "short knife waiting in ambush," bridging the gap between "Me and you—two / Orphans / The smile of two generations." Observation of nature and life ultimately drives Ling Yü's poetic output. Ling Yü does not tell which genres and forms inspire her, but a footnote to "Cactus" notes that Hsi Muren (Xi Murong), an interlocutor, sent her some newspaper clippings of an old poem she had forgotten was "published way back in *United Daily News*'s literary supplement." Ling Yü dialogues, too, with poet-daughters of her generation, just as Hiroshige's Tōkaidō series (1838–39) after the first one features each print with a comic *kyōka* [wild song] poem with vulgar humor, showing his interaction with poets of his time (Forrer 2017: 62; 66; Oka 1982: 38). Reading *Daughters*, we float, guided by Ling Yü's poetic daughters in the big sea, where there's "no opposite shore / The opposite shore is an imaginative pretext."

Nicholas Y. H. Wong
October 2024

Bibliography

Forrer, Matthi. 2017. *Hiroshige*. New York and London: Prestel Publishing.
Oka, Isaburo. 1982. *Hiroshige: Great Japanese Art*. Translated by Stanleigh H. Jones. Tokyo and New York: Kodansha.
Salter, Rebecca. 2006. *Japanese Popular Prints: From Votive Slips to Playing Cards*. Honolulu: University of Hawai'i Press.
Uhlenbeck, Chris and Marije Jansen. 2008. *Hiroshige: Shaping the Image of Japan*. Leiden: Hotei Publishing.

Acknowledgments

In March 2024, Silvia Marijnissen convened a week-long translation workshop of Ling Yü's poems at Translation House Looren in Wernetshausen near Zurich. Participants gave Ling Yü's Chinese an afterlife in Dutch, English, German, and Italian. Besides Silvia, Cosima Bruno, Alice Grünfelder, Wen-chi Li, Rosa Lombardi, Silvia Schiavi, Yu-sheng Tsou, Dylan K. Wang, and Tony Yu provided such stimulating company and helped me rethink some of my translations. I thank the staff at Translation House Looren for their tremendous hospitality and dedication to translation work around the globe. Without the support of the HKU-100 Start-up Fund, and of my home department, the School of Chinese, Faculty of Arts, The University of Hong Kong, I couldn't have rendered *Daughters* and its deep feelings with a carefree mind.

About the Translator

NICHOLAS Y. H. WONG is Assistant Professor in the School of Chinese at the University of Hong Kong. He teaches Chinese-English translation and researches Southeast Asian Chinese writing. He holds a PhD in Comparative Literature from the University of Chicago. Born in Malaysia, he has lived in Singapore and the United States. As Zhou Sivan, he has published three poetry chapbooks.

www.ingramcontent.com/pod-product-compliance
Lightning Source LLC
Chambersburg PA
CBHW030303100526
44590CB00012B/502